To Eileen,

love from.
Nancy.

MEDITATIONS
ON
PEACE

SISTER
WENDY BECKETT

DORLING KINDERSLEY

LONDON • NEW YORK • STUTTGART

A DORLING KINDERSLEY BOOK

*For my dearest mother, with
very great love and gratitude.*

Editor *Patricia Wright*
Art editor *Claire Legemah*
Managing editor *Sean Moore*
Picture researcher *Jo Walton*
Production controller *Alison Jones*

First published in Great Britain in 1995 by
Dorling Kindersley Limited
9 Henrietta Street, London WC2E 8PS

Copyright © 1995 Dorling Kindersley Limited
Text copyright © 1995 Sister Wendy Beckett

A CIP catalogue record for this book is available
from the British Library.

ISBN 075130236 8

Colour reproduction by GRB Edtirice s.r.l.
Printed and bound in Hong Kong by Imago.

CONTENTS

PEACE IMAGINED

EACE IS ONE OF OUR deepest needs, but it does not come just for the wishing. Yet even images of it comfort us. Pictures of unspoiled countryside make visual what many people see as the essence of peace. In Constable's *Cornfield* the sun shines, the fruitful fields wait patiently for the reaper, water is sweet and unpolluted, and the animal world is in harmony with the human. Nowhere is there disturbance or annoyance, no raucous noises, no pressures. This is peace as it may appear in our imagination.

The Cornfield, 1826, John Constable
143 x 122 cm (56¹/₄ x 48 in), oil on canvas
National Gallery, London

AN IDEAL WORLD

THE PERFECT COUNTRYSIDE, the wonderful image of peace, is, of course, as imaginary as the perfect city. An unknown artist from Florence saw the ideal city as supremely beautiful and spacious, with large, gracious buildings existing in compatibility. It is a view that uplifts the heart; but the ideal city is uninhabited. Once human beings come onto the scene, with their clutter and noise, this gentle image of peace would be

destroyed. But we misunderstand the nature of peace if we think of it as an ideal world, or as dependent on silence or solitude: we have, sooner or later, to admit reality – with all its in-built anxieties.

Perspective of an Ideal City, c.1470, Unknown Florentine artist
60 x 200 cm (23¹/₂ x 78³/₄ in), oil on wood panel
Palazzo Ducale, Urbino

CONDITIONAL PEACE

BELLINI'S ALLEGORIES are not always easy to interpret, but this one clearly has as its theme uncertainty, inconstancy, and insecurity. The globe balances precariously on the woman's knee, and its real support is the child, as likely as all the other children to grow tired of the task and take to frolicking. Any peace that rests upon externals is in such a state of insecurity. A good digestion, no financial trouble, happy relationships, an interesting career: then the world is beautiful to us, the children smile, and we are at peace. But of what value is such a peace? At any moment accident or natural change may disrupt it. A peace dependent on the woman's knee remaining still and the diligence of a small child in persisting in its Atlas-stance is a poor, uncertain peace: we cannot be peaceful in a dependence.

Allegory: Inconstancy, c.1490, Giovanni Bellini
33 x 22 cm (13 x 8¹/₂ in), oil on wood panel
Accademia, Venice

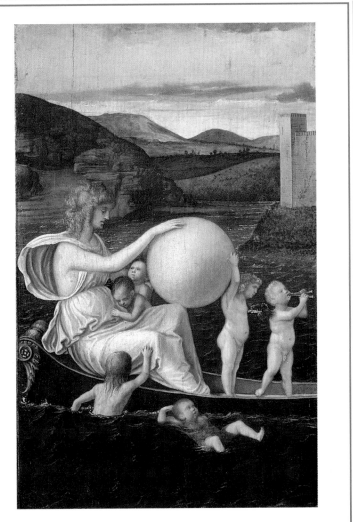

TRANQUILITY

PEACE THAT DEMANDS unreal conditions is a deception. There is no life without work, anxieties, or tensions. Peace is not found in avoiding these but in understanding them and controlling their force. One of the most tranquil faces in art is Raphael's St Nicholas, an intensely active bishop. The stories about his miracles may be legends, but they attest to his great reputation for practical involvement in the personal distresses of his people. Even here, Raphael shows him, not lost in silent prayer, but reading, with his crozier upright in his hand. The unmistakable inner peace we can see has nothing at all to do with an unstressed life; it comes from his insight into the significance of those stresses, their value and their motivation.

St Nicholas of Bari, (detail from the Ansidei Madonna), 1505, Raphael
209.5 x 148.5 cm (82¹/₂ x 58¹/₂ in), oil on wood panel
National Gallery, London

A MEANINGFUL LIFE

WE LONG FOR reassurance, our own personal angelic visit, the removal of obstacles, the certainty of fulfilment. Botticelli's Virgin sways in prayerful wonder as she receives the blessed summons. What will follow? For Mary it will be a life of loneliness and poverty, with her son dying a criminal's death and the only solace her faith. Human strengths can only lead to human satisfactions, and even these are vulnerable to fortune. But these are meagre goals, not enough to lead us into peace. There is no lasting peace that does not rest

upon a sense of life's having meaning. For Mary, that meaning was her divine son; for others, it can come from a determination to do what is right, and the solid certainty that this is something that nobody can wrest away from us.

Annunciation, 1489-90, Sandro Botticelli
150 x 156 cm (59 x 61¹/₂ in), tempera on wood panel
Uffizi Gallery, Florence

CONTEMPLATION

PARADOXICALLY, THE WAY to peace is not to seek it, but to seek selflessness. Self-seeking of any kind narrows our potential and destroys the balance on which peace depends. (We must want totality and accept our helplessness to attain it.) Signorelli is not attempting to show us peace in this detail from *The Circumcision*. He is attempting to be truthful, which does not mean naturalistic accuracy but truth to his own vision. In this single-minded pursuit, which leaves no room for the ego, Signorelli has, as an artistic by-product, given us a view of inner peace. These two attendants at the circumcision are not actively involved, but are engrossed in their contemplative role. Their identity is unimportant: in this drama they are onlookers, and they look on with loving concentration. Their peace comes from their response to the actual, unselfconscious and entire.

Two Heads (detail from The Circumcision), c.1491, Luca Signorelli
285.5 x 180 cm (101³/₄ x 71 in), oil on wood panel
National Gallery, London

FINDING A BALANCE

TRUE PEACE, dependent on nothing external, and hence wholly steadfast, comes from an inner balance between desire and potential. As long as we hunger for what we cannot have and battle hopelessly against what must always defeat us, we are not at peace. In case this sounds discouraging, the point is that it is not so much that we cannot have all we desire – and more – but that we have to align our desires in the truth. Our spirit is too great for small and specific happinesses: our potential is infinite. The secret of peace is determining where this infinitude is, and here is where the need for balance becomes paramount. In this painting Mondrian has used only three colours and a few black lines, and from their balance created a painting of the most subtle passion. Move a line or modify a rectangle, and the balance is lost and the painting becomes dull.

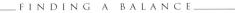

Composition in Red, Yellow and Blue, 1930, Piet Mondrian
51 x 51 cm (20 x 20), oil on canvas
Private collection

A FLUID STILLNESS

BALANCE IS RARELY mathematical or rigorous. *The Book of Kells* is a celebration of Celtic graphic invention, an intricate marvel of interlace and astonishing complexities. Yet it is even more astonishing in its mysterious balance. It is not a balance of complementaries: the strange human figure at the top right has no counterpart. The page spells out the opening words of St Mark's gospel in Latin, (*Initium evengelii IHU XPI*), and most of the space is devoted to the great verticals of the 'N' of the first word. But twist and intertwine as they will, the pattern maintains a stillness, and a purity of balance. Within the movement then, is a deep and satisfying peace.

Opening words of St Mark's Gospel, Book of Kells, c.800
33 x 24 cm (13 x 9¹/₂ in), tempera
Trinity College, Dublin

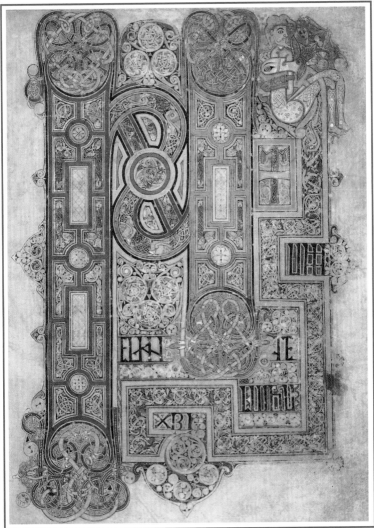

VISUAL PRAYER

THE UNDERSTANDING that peace is the result of an inner balance is what makes this leaf from the Koran so contemplative in its grace. It is written in Kufic script, a wonder of calligraphy, which was created to do due honour to the Word of Allah, and its grand curves, swoops and blotches have an integral harmony peculiar to themselves. The calligrapher has used all his resources – precious ink and artistic sense of patterning – but he has also sought something beyond human resources: a visual prayer, a sacred affirmation of the Holy. Because he has grasped that the objective is beyond human power, the calligrapher has aimed only in the direction of that objective, offering fallibility as a means to achievement; and the miracle has happened.

Leaf from the Koran, (date unknown)
21.5 x 11.5 cm (8¹/₂ x 4¹/₂ in), ink on paper
Musée Conde, Chantilly

وَلَقَدْ قَالُوا كَلِمَةَ الْكُفْرِ وَكَفَرُوا بَعْدَ
إِسْلَامِهِمْ وَهَمُّوا بِمَا لَمْ يَنَالُوا وَمَا نَقَمُوا
إِلَّا أَنْ أَغْنَاهُمُ اللَّهُ وَرَسُولُهُ مِنْ فَضْلِهِ فَإِنْ
يَتُوبُوا يَكُ خَيْرًا لَهُمْ وَإِنْ يَتَوَلَّوْا يُعَذِّبْهُمُ
اللَّهُ عَذَابًا أَلِيمًا فِي الدُّنْيَا وَالْآخِرَةِ وَمَا لَهُمْ
فِي الْأَرْضِ مِنْ وَلِيٍّ وَلَا نَصِيرٍ وَمِنْهُمْ مَنْ
عَاهَدَ اللَّهَ لَئِنْ آتَانَا مِنْ فَضْلِهِ لَنَصَّدَّقَنَّ
وَلَنَكُونَنَّ مِنَ الصَّالِحِينَ فَلَمَّا آتَاهُمْ مِنْ
فَضْلِهِ بَخِلُوا بِهِ وَتَوَلَّوْا وَهُمْ مُعْرِضُونَ
فَأَعْقَبَهُمْ نِفَاقًا فِي قُلُوبِهِمْ إِلَى يَوْمِ
يَلْقَوْنَهُ بِمَا أَخْلَفُوا اللَّهَ مَا وَعَدُوهُ وَبِمَا
كَانُوا يَكْذِبُونَ أَلَمْ يَعْلَمُوا أَنَّ اللَّهَ يَعْلَمُ

HUMAN FAILURE

WE CANNOT CONTROL our life. If we are set upon doing so, we have abdicated from peace, which must balance what is desired with what is possible. As Hokusai shows so memorably, the great wave is in waiting for any boat. It is unpredictable, as uncontrollable now as it was at the dawn of time. Will the slender boats survive or will they be overwhelmed? The risk is a human constant; it has to be accepted – and laid aside. What we can do, we do. Beyond that, we endure, our endurance framed by a sense of what matters and what does not. The worst is not that we may be overwhelmed by disaster, but to fail to live by principle. Yet we are fallible, and so the real worst, the antithesis of peace, is to refuse to recognise failure and humbly begin again.

The Great Wave, 1831, Katsushika Hokusai
25 x 36 cm (9³/₄ x 14 in), ink on paper
Private collection

COURAGE

GILLES IS A MAN discomforted: he stands exposed, tense and unhappy. Yet we could not call him a man who is not at peace. Something has happened (Watteau does not spell it out) that has removed him from his fellow actors and left him painfully alone. Gilles is ill at ease, but he has no option: what is happening must be lived through, and he sets himself to do it. This courage – this acceptance of powerlessness and decision to await consequences from which we cannot escape – this is an element of peacefulness. Gilles is at peace because he does not rage against the inevitable. The wisdom is in knowing what is inevitable and what, with courage and intelligence, can be changed. Fundamentally though, nothing matters except to be true to what we know is right.

Gilles, 1721, Jean-Antoine Watteau
184.5 x 149.5 cm (72$\frac{1}{2}$ x 59 in), oil on canvas
Musée du Louvre, Paris

THE BLESSING OF PEACE

THERE IS NOTHING passive about peace. Like Crivelli's child, we must always peer around obstacles, never accepting that our vision is limited until we have tried to see to the furthest horizons. We look, we ponder, we revolve possible alternatives. Then, we submit, either to what seems possible or to what seems inevitable. If we have planned with our eyes focused on what is right, then failure is not all that important. It is painful, but it is not destructive. (A child is hardly an image of peace because it does not yet understand the relative insignificance of success or of failure.) The blessing of peace, then, is in knowing that we have only to do what we morally can, and then live without repining in the outcome. Those we love die, possessions are stolen or diminished: only goodness remains. Yet however terrible our suffering, it will not last eternally. On that condition is based our peace.

Detail from The Annunciation, 1486, Carlo Crivelli
207 x 146.5 cm (81¹/₂ x 57³/₄ in), oil on wood (transferred to canvas)
National Gallery, London

THE ILLUSION OF PEACE

GOOD IS NOT a judgement we can make about ourselves. We instinctively react against Ingres' young Marquis, who so obviously has a high opinion of himself. Whether he considers himself virtuous is not spelt out, but he stands before us with the restrained smirk of self-admiration. Those who are genuinely good, always doubt it. Peace does not depend upon anything, certainly not upon our own certainty of moral righteousness. It depends upon humble desire (with the emphasis on humble) to do what is right. Ingres' sitter, decorations prominent, simplicity of attire elegantly visible, hands electric with a sense of superiority, has a totally dependent kind of peace. Humiliation and failure would explode it, whereas true peace is impervious to events. Peace rests upon the decision always to struggle towards goodness, whatever our condition. In this light, one feels compassion for Amédée-David, with all his spiritual disadvantages.

Amédée-David, Marquis de Pastoret, 1826
Jean-Auguste-Dominique Ingres
103 x 82 cm (40¹/₂ x 32³/₄ in), oil on canvas
Art Institute of Chicago

A BRIGHT FORTRESS

THERE IS AN IMMENSE freedom in peace. Because it needs no external support, it can take all risks that seem wise to it. Pia Stern's *Seaside Residence* shows a structure, (a "residence") on the very edge of the waves. They surge relentlessly towards it, almost, it seems, engulfing it; yet the structure stands. The unpredictability of the furrowed water, swaying inexorably inward, does not substantially affect the "residence". It is a bright fortress, that apparently exists by other principles. If wild water is black-and-white, then the human home of the spirit is luminous with colour, bright enough to reflect onto the incoming waves, though not to deflect them. Stern shows us two ways of being: the physical, answerable only to accident, to wind and tide; and the spiritual, answerable to an inward sense of truth. One is free-flowing; the other is fixed, grounded in more than its own small compass – in God.

Seaside Residence II, 1994, Pia Stern
21 x 20.5 cm (8¹/₄ x 8 in), pastel on paper
Private collection

CHOOSING PEACE

AN ACCEPTANCE OF the vulnerability on which peace is based, and the weighing up of significance in the light of eternity, can seem to some an abdication from life's everyday realities. Hammershoi's woman sits in an enclosed space, head bent. She could be thought to be imprisoned by her context and weakly complicit with her lack of liberty. Yet the artist shows us door upon door, with a luminous window beyond. Light plays over the woman's form from behind as well as from ahead. If she chooses, she has only to stand erect and move down the waiting corridor. If she stays motionless (reading? sewing?), that is her choice. Peace is never imposed; it cannot be. It is a deliberate choice, an ordering of priorities in a moral context. We look at the options and evaluate them.

Interior, 1908, Vilhelm Hammershøi
79 x 66 cm (31 x 26 in), oil on canvas
Aarhus Kunstmuseum

ISOLATION

THE SAFETY OF PEACE has nothing at all to do with aloofness from other people, keeping oneself free from the risk of emotional pain. Carel Weight's *The Silence* shows three people, almost three generations, motionless, silent, enclosed in their walled space, protected against the outside world and one another. Not one of them is at peace. They sit or stand stiffly, coldly, worryingly remote from family closeness. To isolate oneself is not to be at peace, and makes the acceptance of true life (which peace entails), impossible. Peace does not reject our longings, it is warm, not cold: a passionate commitment to becoming a full person. This means sacrificing the neat goals of the fantasy person, one of which is that it is possible to live fruitfully in hostile isolation from our fellows.

The Silence, 1965, Carel Weight
91.5 x 122 cm (36 x 48 in), oil on board
Royal Academy of Arts, London

JOURNEY TO PEACE

PEACE COMES FROM unselfishly doing what is right. St George has two options: kill the dragon (the rapacity and cruelty within him), or let it ravage. He chooses to kill, and Albert Herbert shows him at the bottom of the picture, vulnerably exposed but triumphant, the deed done. Jonah had no option: the whale engulfed him. His choice then was to lie within its belly until circumstances opened a path to the light. It was not a passive waiting,

St George and the Dragon, Jonah in the Whale, and the House of God
1990–91, Albert Herbert
66 x 21.5 cm (26 x 8¹/₂ in), oil on wood
Private collection

but a thoughtful one, working out why this had happened and what use he could make of it. The top image, the house of God, exceeds the panel, as if this house can never be confined within man-made boundaries. The house stands open, a rich, bright red visible within. Herbert invites us to identify with the two bystanders: will they enter the solid protection of the house? No moral judgement is made, merely a series of existential possibilities. Peace exists on all three levels.

REDEMPTION

NO IMAGE OF PEACE has ever been more powerful or more encouraging than that of Christ as he faced his passion. He knew that in a short time he would be betrayed by a close friend and that his death would be a terrible one – crucifixion. He would die with his work barely begun, and the sense of failure must have been crushing. He must, too, have felt rejection: why had God, his Father, not protected him? The stained glass painting of this scene is particularly moving, because the thick lead supports, which the glass technically needs, isolate Jesus from comfort, and from his friends lost in sleep around him. He is alone. We are told Jesus was in an agony of grief and fear, yet he was equally in a state of the most profound peace. He did not understand, but he trusted, and would go to death trusting. Peace may not expel terrible emotions, but it underlies them and makes them – as with Christ – redemptive.

The Agony in the Garden, 1441, Hans Acker
104 x 62 cm (41 x 24¹/₂ in), stained glass
The Besserrer Chapel, Ulm Cathedral

INDEX

PICTURE CREDITS

*Every effort has been made to trace the copyright holders and we
apologise in advance for any unintentional omissions. We would be
pleased to insert the appropriate acknowledgement in any subsequent
edition of this publication.*

Endpapers Reproduced by
courtesy of the Trustees of
the National Gallery, London
p5 Reproduced by courtesy
of the Trustees of the
National Gallery, London
p7 Christies, London/
Bridgeman Art Library
p9 Reproduced by courtesy
of the Trustees of the
National Gallery, London
pp10-11 Palazzo Ducale,
Urbino/Scala
p13 Accademia, Venice/Scala
p15 Reproduced by
courtesy of the Trustees of
the National Gallery, London
pp16-17 Uffizi Gallery,
Florence/Scala
p19 Reproduced by
courtesy of the Trustees of
the National Gallery, London
p21 Christies London/
Bridgeman Art Library/©
1995 ABC/Mondrian
Estate/Holtzman Trust.
Licensed by ILP
p23 The Board of Trinity
College Dublin
p25 Musée Conde,
Chantilly/Giraudon
pp26-27 Christies, London/
Bridgeman Art Library
p29 Musée du Louvre,
Paris/©Photo R.M.N.
p31 Reproduced by
courtesy of the Trustees of
the National Gallery, London
p33 Bequest of Dorothy
Eckhart Williams; Robert
Allerton Purchase, Bertha

E. Brown, and Major
Acquisitions funds,
1971.452, photo ©1995, The
Art Institute of Chicago,
All Rights Reserved
p35 Courtesy of the artist
p37 Aarhus Kunstmuseum
pp38-39 Royal Academy
of Arts, London
pp40-41 Private collection,
Courtesy England & Co
Gallery, London
p43 The Besserrer Chapel,
Ulm Cathedral/©Sonia
Halliday and Laura
Lushington

JACKET PICTURE CREDITS

Benozzo di Lese
*The Virgin and Child Enthroned
among Angels and Saints
(detail)*

Master of Liesborn
*Saints Cosmas and Damian
and the Virgin (detail)*

Style of Orcagna
*Small Altarpiece: The
Crucifixion (detail)*

Reproduced by courtesy of
the Trustees of the National
Gallery, London